Cryptocurrency

Learn Everything You Need To Know About Bitcoin, The
Original And Most Important Cryptocurrency

*(How To Mine Cryptocurrency Like A Pro: A Guide To
Unlocking The Secrets)*

Stanislaw Dobler

TABLE OF CONTENT

Taking Note Of The Breakout

Until now, we have discussed the concept of trading inside a range. If you choose the correct stocks and keep an eye out for patterns, you can make a lot of money doing that, and it's also a sort of trading that has a relatively low risk and requires little work on your part.

But if you want to make it big time, you need the overwhelming profits that come with a breakthrough. This is the only way to get there. Do you remember the analogy I made when I was discussing the share price and the trendline, when I compared it to a "ball on a rubber band"? When the rubber band snaps, what happens? That's what we call a breakout: the ball travels far, way up into the air (although, of course, if we're talking about stocks, it might also go in the opposite direction)! Trading a breakout is analogous to getting on a train after it has already

1

begun going, as compared to trading inside a range, which is like trading within a confined area.

Simply to let you know: A breakout is the process of breaking out of a pattern, and it may take place in either the up or the down direction.

On the other side, the only direction a breakdown can go is downward.

Launch of operation

When a stock price swings outside of an established channel, support, or resistance line in conjunction with increasing volume, this is referred to be a breakout. This is a little more technical way of describing what happens. (The higher trading volume is necessary to demonstrate that it is not only a coincidence but rather a genuine breakout.) The price follows the breakout to the upside, and it does so quite quickly.

A true breakthrough requires making a significant and risky action. If you check at a chart made using candlesticks, you'll see that the price of the asset has closed much higher than the resistance level. If all you notice is the price slightly beyond the level of resistance, then what you are seeing is not a genuine breakout; rather, it is a fakeout. It's a fakeout if the price is going close to the resistance line but hasn't broken through it yet. Keep an eye out for this scenario. Hold off on making any trades until the line has been breached.

There won't be as many breakouts to trade, but stocks that have the strength to move against the market are stocks that should really get going once they start, so you will still get that speedy rise even in a bear market. By the way, a breakout can occur even in a market that is in a major downtrend.

Your signal is really straightforward: when the price first breaks out of the channel, or when it breaks the resistance line, and then closes above it.

How does the process of breakouts work? One of the tactics they use is something that's known as a lockout rally. Imagine you hold a well-known stock that has been doing poorly for the last several years; the company has taken some corrective measures, and the stock price has leveled out; but, it has not yet started to move in an upward direction.

Everyone is anticipating that it will soon be time to purchase it once again; yet, nobody has really done so since they are waiting for something. And for whatever reason you get a little purchasing — maybe one bold fund manager, perhaps a couple of brokers jumping in — and it goes through the line, and now all those people who haven't purchased it have a big sensation of FOMO (which, as case you didn't know, means Fear of Missing Out). And this drives up the price of the stock. Because it is driving, it must be time to buy, so they purchase, which causes the price to go up a little bit more, which encourages even more people to buy...

Naturally, short-term traders will have already cashed in their winnings at that time and will be exiting the market.

Cryptocurrencies Have Both Positives And Negatives To Offer

Cryptocurrencies provide various benefits over traditional currencies, traditional banking systems, and traditional methods of transferring money. However, just like any other financial tools and vehicles, digital currencies come with their own unique set of challenges and risks. Let's talk about how cryptocurrencies work, as well as the benefits and drawbacks involved with using them.

In favor of Privacy

The term "crypto," which comes from the Greek word for "hidden" or "secret," inspired the developers of cryptocurrencies to construct a mechanism that would disguise the identity of both the person sending and receiving cryptocurrency cash.

They place a high value on the confidentiality of their customers' information. Only cryptocurrency can provide the same level of privacy as cash transactions.

A lack of abundance

One of the most widely used currencies, Bitcoin, is limited to a predetermined quantity. There are already over seventeen million Bitcoins in circulation, but there will only ever be twenty-one million total Bitcoins. Because of this restricted supply, Bitcoin and other cryptocurrencies have features with precious metals like silver and gold that have historically been used for monetary purposes. In contrast, the supply of any fiat currency (such as the United States Dollar and the British Pound), once it is in circulation, will never increase again; as a result, the purchasing power of the currency will decrease.

A move away from centralized control

The owners of cryptocurrencies must utilize a digital wallet in order to access their digital money, transfer or receive payments from a specific wallet address, and apply a secret key in order to get access to their cash. Although there are some owners who like the practice of storing their assets in an exchange, doing so exposes them to an additional danger.

The record of the money may be found on the blockchain, and a duplicate of the record is preserved on each full node, which is a computer that locally holds a ledger and synchronizes with other computers online.

To put it another way, your money is not just kept in a single bank or many institutions. The information is stored in a remote location and replicated around the globe to all complete nodes. Because bitcoin ledgers are decentralized, digital assets are less likely to be lost or stolen as a result of locally focused threats or seizures, such as a malfunction in a piece of hardware or a fire.

Intelligent Contracts

Some cryptocurrencies are equipped with a one-of-a-kind quality that cannot be replicated using traditional forms of currency.

The cryptocurrency known as Ethereum is an excellent illustration of this category. It provides robust support for smart contracts, which are computer programs that may be used to handle transactions and live on a distributed ledger called blockchain. At their core, these contracts are able to function in lieu of escrow services and arbitrators. The particulars of a transaction are handled by the smart contract, which holds off on releasing payment until certain predetermined criteria have been attained.

Transferring Expenses

The cost that is connected with transfers may either be a benefit or a burden depending on the kind of cryptocurrency being transferred, the method of transfer being used, and the transfer speed. For instance, if you choose a fast clearing for a specific transaction, the cost of Bitcoin will skyrocket to an unreasonably high level. Transfers that are less time-sensitive will result in lower costs and fewer complications.

Ripple is yet another cryptocurrency that allows for cheap and speedy transactions thanks to its decentralized network. Because of this, financial institutions favor the deployment of technology and transactions associated to Ripple more than other options.

Cons

Investors need to be aware that cryptocurrencies come with a set of factors to make for safer investments in order to make informed decisions. One should be aware that there is currently no cryptocurrency that can be considered safe since it is still in its early stages.

Despite this, it is possible to construct a portfolio that keeps risks to a minimum while yet giving you the flexibility to get

out of a transaction when it becomes
necessary.

What Exactly Is A Blockchain, Anyway?

In a nutshell, a blockchain is the comprehensive and immutable record of all the transactions that have ever taken place inside a decentralized community. This record is accepted by all members of the community. This ledger is maintained on every participant's computer, is automatically updated at certain intervals, and is acknowledged by the community as a reliable source of information. since of this, there is no need for a single party to control the society since nobody will be able to spend the same amount again. That would immediately result in a disagreement being recorded in the transaction history of each participant.

The community, as opposed to an authoritative third party, determines what constitutes "reality" in a way that is decentralized. The use of blockchain technology makes it possible to store any form of "reality" without the intervention of a central authority. This may be used to any kind of ownership, identity, knowledge, or even cash, depending on the context.

NOMENCLATURE RELATING TO BLOCKCHAINS AND CRYPTOCURRENCIES

For the sake of clarity, let's take a moment to clarify a few terms:

A decentralized community's transaction history, stored in an immutable ledger called blockchain.

The term "cryptocurrency" refers to a program that makes use of blockchain technology. This application stores the transaction history and, as a result, the precise quantity of currency that each individual has through a blockchain.

The term "Bitcoin" (with a capital "B") refers to both the concept and the protocol that underpins the world's first decentralized cryptocurrency built on a blockchain. Bitcoins, with a lowercase b: the name given to the money itself.

As an example, consider the following: "Thomas is aware of cryptocurrencies, but rather than being enthusiastic about a single application, he is more interested in the blockchain." Still, Thomas has 12.7 bitcoins in his possession because he is optimistic about the future worth of the cryptocurrency and since he discovered that investing in the blockchain itself was not viable.

A Concluding Assessment

There is no one trading method that stands out above the others; rather, each approach caters to a different set of requirements. Day trading offers a greater opportunity for profit, at any rate in terms of the rate of return on smaller anticipated trading accounts. In a certain sense, swing traders have a far better chance of maintaining the rate of return on their investments even as their accounts grow in size.

The minimum required amounts of capital are subject to significant movement across the many different trading techniques and marketplaces. Day trading demands more time than swing trading does, but mastering any strategy requires a significant amount of practice to become consistent. Day training is the finest option for those who like doing active things. Swing trading is an option that requires less effort and less time commitment and is available to those who are seeking for it.

The star Stellar (Xlm)

Stellar is an open blockchain network that joins financial institutions for the purpose of large-scale transactions and offers solutions for businesses. Huge exchanges between financial institutions like as banks and investment companies, which would traditionally take several days, include a number of mediators, and command a significant amount of money, may now be completed relatively instantly with no middlemen and control very little or nothing at all for those who are conducting the trade.

Stellar has positioned itself as an enterprise

blockchain for institutional trading; however, despite this positioning, it is still an open blockchain and anybody may use it. The architecture makes it possible to conduct transactions across borders using any currency. Lumens (XLM) is the native currency of the Stellar network.16 For users to be able to conduct transactions on the web, the network requires them to have Lumens.

Jed McCaleb, who was also a founding member of Ripple Labs and the creator of the Ripple protocol, is the person responsible for the creation of Stellar. After some time, he decided to leave his job at Ripple and help form the Stellar

Development Foundation instead.

As of November 2021, one Stellar Lumen is valued at $0.33 and the demand capitalization for this cryptocurrency is at $8 billion.18

Doge, short for dogecoin,

The price of Dogecoin, which many people consider

to be the first "meme coin," surged in 2021, which sparked a commotion in the cryptocurrency market. A number of well-known businesses, such as the Dallas Mavericks and Kronos, as well as SpaceX, an American aerospace corporation owned by Elon Musk, accept payment in the form of the coin, which has an image of a shibainu serving as its avatar.

Dogecoin was first developed in 2013 by two software programmers by the names of Billy Markus and Jackson Palmer. Reportedly, Markus and Palmer created the coin as a joke as a comment on the irrational speculation that has been going on in the cryptocurrency industry.

During the course of the week, the price of DOGE reached an all-time high of $0.71. It was planned that Elon Musk will make an appearance on Saturday Night Live. Dogecoin has a market capitalization of $29.2 billion as of November 2021, and the value of one DOGE is now approximately $0.22. This places it as the tenth-largest cryptocurrency by market capitalization.

Risk Posed By A Counterparty

The faith that people have in their counterparties is essential to the value of the fiat currency. Similar to confidence, trust is an immaterial concept that can only ever be understood on an individual level. In a world where there is objectivity, all of the agreements made between governments and the various central banks, as well as all of those that depend on the various systems of fiat money, are subject to modification and may be violated according to circumstances.

In point of fact, they are almost always violated anytime a currency's value is artificially inflated. All of this money would be rendered useless as a result of the unfulfilled promises made by failing governments and institutions.

The completion of the transaction

A transaction that would be conducted using commodity money would be a straightforward exchange of item of value for another thing of worth. When a transaction involving fiat money is carried out, one party will possess the fiat currency, while the other party will be the beneficiary of all of the goods or services being exchanged.

Due to the fact that the value of the currency might fluctuate at any moment and at times reach zero, this constitutes a backdated breach of the contract. A residual third party will always be involved in the transaction in some capacity. In this case, it would be the government or the central bank, and the transactions themselves would not be resolved.

Rivals or rivals

The terms "BTC and other cryptos" and "supportingcryptocurrencies" will appear several times throughout the text of this book. This is due to the fact that Bitcoin (BTC) does not control the technology that underpins it. There are various applications for blockchain technology, and once bitcoin (BTC) was released, a number of other firms attempted to launch their own cryptocurrencies. This indicates that there is a lot of competition on the cryptocurrency market. Even if Bitcoin (BTC) is the most well-known cryptocurrency at the moment, this does not exclude the possibility of other cryptocurrencies overtaking it.

Alternate cryptocurrencies, or altcoins, were given their moniker when they first debuted on the market after Bitcoin (BTC). Today, the term "altcoin" refers to any and all cryptocurrencies that are in direct competition with Bitcoin. There is a sprinkling of meme culture that surrounds BTC's rivals. These memes encapsulate the controversy and the background of the situation in lighthearted, bite-sized chunks. The story that is told about this culture is that these currencies have supporters and representatives who swear by them, only for those supporters to wind up losing money, but the past is considerably more complicated than that narrative suggests. In the realm of commerce, payment systems that take Bitcoin into mind also take into consideration a variety of other cryptocurrencies. It's a win-win situation for the kind of applications in question: If they support a single technology, they will be able to collect transaction fees regardless of the cryptocurrency that is being used.

The following is a list of the most significant rivals to Bitcoin, along with some information on them:

Ethereum is a peer-to-peer (P2P) network that runs decentralized software. The fact that Ethereum, also known by its acronym ETH, may be used all around the world, similar to Bitcoin, is one of the reasons why it is so popular. It may be purchased without the need of having a bank account, and everyone, regardless of their history, has unrestricted access to it. The fundamental principles that underpin it remain the same. Its price has increased dramatically in recent times, and it now sits in second position, after Bitcoin.

Litecoin was one of the first cryptocurrencies to emerge after Bitcoin and was introduced in 2011 when it was developed by Charlie Lee. It is a peer-to-peer (P2P) decentralized virtual currency like Bitcoin (BTC), but the technology behind it allows for transactions to be completed more quickly. To this day, it remains one of the most widely used cryptocurrencies in circulation.

Dogecoin is an open-source cryptocurrency that was introduced in 2013. It was called after the "doge meme," which became popular in the cryptocurrency world around the same time. The face of the meme, which is a

ShibaInu dog seeming confused, is included on the company's logo. The fact that Dogecoin, often known as DOGE for its abbreviated form, was first intended as a joke is an intriguing fact about the cryptocurrency. Despite this, it established itself as a viable option in the online market. It is still used as a form of tipping cash for content on social media platforms, which accounts for its widespread usage on Reddit and Twitter.

XRP, which is owned by Ripple, is a cryptocurrency that was created by the firm Ripple. At first, it provided peer-to-peer (P2P) financial services that let individuals to borrow money without first going through a financial institution such as a bank or another company. In 2012, they devised XRP with the intention of using it as a bridge currency between two other currencies whose values were different from one another. Although it has quicker processing times and reduced transaction fees, it is not a public blockchain-based currency like Bitcoin (BTC).

Binance Coin: Created by the cryptocurrency trading platform Binance, Binance Coin, also known as BNB, operates on the Ethereumblockchain and has a hard cap of just 200 Million BNB that may be mined. It was developed as an incentive for customers of Binance to use their services as well as an incentive for miners to contribute to the Binance ecosystem.

Secure by tethering: Even though it is a stablecoin (a term used to describe cryptocurrencies that are backed by a reserve asset), it is in direct competition with Bitcoin. It is supported by both the Japanese yen and the United States dollar. The reserves that support Tether (USDT) are held in banks throughout the world. In terms of the technology behind blockchains, it is comparable to Bitcoin. Because of its lower rate of volatility in comparison to decentralized cryptocurrencies, it is quite popular among investors.

ETH was supposed to be replaced by Cardano (ADA), which was founded by one of the early members of ETH, Charles Hoskinson, after the two parties got into a disagreement over something. In order to get an advantage over its rival, the team of researchers behind ADA conducted one of the most extensive investigations of the blockchain technology.

Polkadot: In a manner similar to that of ADA, Polkadot (DOT) was developed by Gavin Wood, an additional member of the founding team of ETH. It applies blockchain and proof-of-stake technologies in a comparable manner.

The Probable Course Of Events For Bitcoin And Other Cryptocurrencies

There is a lot of uncertainty about what the future holds for bitcoin. According to Kenneth Rogoff, a professor at Harvard University, the total market value of cryptocurrencies may see a large growth over the course of the next five years. In point of fact, he estimates that it will climb to between $5 trillion and $10 trillion.

He goes on to argue that the true worth of one Bitcoin throughout its whole lifespan may actually end up being far lower than the 100,000 dollars that some people assume it will be. After all, the usage of Bitcoin is restricted to ordinary transactions; as a result, it is susceptible to a collapse similar to that of a bubble.

In addition to this, the procedure of verifying Bitcoin transactions is not particularly effective. Despite the fact that it has a long history of volatility, he says there is no need for alarm at this time.

If you still wish to invest in Bitcoin and take advantage of the anonymity and decentralization it provides for transactions, you should be aware that government agencies are increasing their level of scrutiny toward the cryptocurrency. This should not come as a surprise given that criminals prefer to utilize it for their unlawful operations such as the distribution of illegal drugs, the laundering of illicit funds, the acquisition of illegal firearms, and smuggling illegal goods.

You should also be aware of its limits, such as its susceptibility to being hacked or crashing your computer. Hackers have the ability to empty virtual bank accounts when they get access to them. On the other hand, technological advancement is often progressive through time. Therefore, more advanced technology in the future may make it possible to increase the security of virtual bank accounts.

You don't only need to keep an eye on Bitcoin; there are other cryptocurrencies as well. Every cryptocurrency runs the risk of being subjected to an increased level of government scrutiny and regulation, which might ultimately lead to the end of their existence.

Additionally, despite the fact that an increasing number of businesses are beginning to acknowledge cryptocurrencies as a form of payment, such establishments are still in the minority. It is necessary for there to be a greater level of acceptance of this digital currency among consumers and businesses before it can become more widely utilized.

One may conclude that it is simpler for younger people to adjust to the changes brought about by current technology breakthroughs. But what about those who aren't as adept when it comes to technology? Sadly, a large number of individuals continue to find bitcoin difficult to understand and difficult to work with. Therefore, it is possible that they will be dissuaded from using it.

Any cryptocurrency that aspires to be a part of the mainstream financial system is going to have to prove that it satisfies a broad variety of requirements. For instance, they need to be sufficiently complicated to maintain their security against cybercriminals and fraudsters. On the other hand, they have to be user-friendly to the point where they are easy to comprehend.

Additionally, cryptocurrencies need to be decentralized while yet providing a sufficient amount of safety and protection for users. They should also be able to protect the privacy of users while avoiding becoming a conduit for criminal activities such as money laundering and evading taxes.

Alternate Forms of Bitcoin

Bitcoin is a name that needs no introduction to

cryptocurrencyenthusiasts since everyone has at least heard of it. Since it was first made available to the general public, it has rapidly evolved into a method of payment that is widely accepted. However, at the current time, businesses have begun to acknowledge the existence of alternative cryptocurrencies.

For example, Litecoin is widely regarded as Bitcoin's most formidable competitor at the present time. It was created with the intention of processing smaller transactions at a quicker rate than Bitcoin. As a matter of fact, it was referred to as the "coin that is silver to Bitcoin's gold."

You may simply mine Litecoin on your desktop computer if it is something you are interested in doing. You got it just perfectly! In contrast to Bitcoin, there is no longer any need for you to obtain cumbersome computer equipment. Even more favorable is the fact that the maximum supply of Litecoin is limited to eighty-four million, while the maximum supply of Bitcoin is just twenty-one million.

You may also want to look into Ripple. It functions as both a method of payment and a kind of money, much as Bitcoin does. Its monetary component is comparable to that of Bitcoin in many ways. It is possible to argue that it is superior thanBitcoin in a number of respects. For instance, its payment method makes it possible to complete the processing of financial transfers in only a few seconds. When paying with Bitcoin, you should anticipate a wait time of several minutes for the same sort of service.

There is also something called MintChip, which functions similarly to Bitcoin in that users are not required to provide any kind of identity to use it. On the other hand, in contrast to other cryptocurrencies, it was developed by a government-backed organization. In contrast to Bitcoin, it is thus supported by actual cash. It is essentially an electronic smartcard that stores value in digital form.

The Creator Class And Non-Founding Types

The epidemic dealt a significant blow to the creative class from a monetary point of view. Artists, musicians, singers, actors, and creators of every variety have been put in the position of having to fend for themselves due to the closure of the typical venues for live performances and exhibits. However, a very fresh (and quite astounding) development took place. The end outcome may be the rise of a creative class that is lucrative, self-sufficient, and independent for the very first time.

The archaic and worn-out image of the "starving artist" has been around for a long time. It is expected that fine artists would not be concerned with mundane matters such as obtaining food or a place to live. They've been "suffering for their art" for hundreds of years now. Because dancers often don't consume a lot of food, no one ever considers them to be "starving dancers." However, the situation is not much better for musicians. Papa Bach served as a church organist in addition to his work as an organ repairman. Mozart was always taking loans out from his family, friends, and acquaintances, despite the fact that he did sometimes earn legitimate income. Although Beethoven did not end his life in abject poverty, he did make a living from commission to commission. There is one thing that every artist has ever had in common with every other artist who has ever lived, and that is that they have all practiced their craft at the pleasure of a patron prior to the year 2021.

The customers

Someone with financial resources has supported almost every artistic endeavor that has ever been undertaken. This funding may have come from a monarch, a wealthy individual, a business, a media firm, a label, a museum, or something else entirely. There are, without a doubt, a few prominent outliers; yet, this does not imply that the rule is wrong. When it comes to contemporary history, the great majority of artists (regardless of the artform they practice) have desired and required something like to a "recording contract with a major label" in order to be able to feed and pay the rent while simultaneously working toward achieving their creative ambitions.

The one who gave birth to inventions

One of the most apparent and rapid pandemic-accelerated digital shifts has taken place inside the creative class. You can be sure that if you go to YouTube, TikTok, Instagram, or any other social video site, you will discover a creator who is fully equipped with direct-to-consumer (DTC) business tools. From payment processing to analytics to production capabilities, practically everything a creative needs to "get paid" is accessible with little to no upfront commitment. This includes the ability to produce content. This is more than just an online version of the traditional practice of passing the hat to support your busking. The growing creative class is being powered, enabled, and will benefit from a large technological infrastructure that is now in the process of being built.

Patreon, a network that links over 200,000 authors with about 7 million users, was valued at $4 billion after its most recent funding round. The company is expected to treble its value by September 2020. Cameo is a website that gives well-known people the ability to deliver tailored films to their devoted followers directly (for a price, of course). OnlyFans is a popular app among both sex workers and others who specialize in physical fitness.

It is vital to recognize that every social video post has become a chance to promote unique material that fans may support, and that all of these applications (as well as hundreds of others) have been purpose-built to allow the reimbursement of artists by their followers.

Protection OfCryptocurrencies

The security of cryptocurrency is composed on two distinct layers. The first component results from the challenging nature of locating hash intersections, which is a task that is performed by miners. The second possibility, which is also the more likely one, is an attack using the "51%" method. In this hypothetical situation, a miner who controls more than 51% of the network's mining power would be in a position to seize control of the global blockchain ledger and produce an alternate block chain. Even at this late stage, the attacker's options for what he can do are restricted. The attacker might either reverse his own transaction or stop other transactions from taking place.

A transaction hold may be placed on a cryptocurrency's account by an acquirer like as PayPal or by law enforcement.

Cryptocurrencies are also susceptible to being seized by law enforcement. All cryptocurrencies provide a level of pseudo-anonymity, and some coins even offer the additional capability of complete anonymity.

Legality and Taxation of Cryptocurrencies • The Taxation of Bitcoin

Despite the fact that cryptocurrencies are legal in most countries, Iceland and Vietnam are the only exceptions; Iceland is an exception mostly owing to the fact that they have placed a freeze on its foreign exchange. However, cryptocurrencies are still subject to regulation and restrictions. Although cryptocurrencies are legal in Russia, it is against the law to buy anything with a currency other than the ruble. China has prohibited financial institutions from dealing with bitcoin, and Russia has legalized cryptocurrencies but made it illegal to buy anything with them.

The Internal Revenue Service (IRS) of the United States has ruled that Bitcoin should be treated as property for the purposes of taxes. This means that Bitcoin is now liable to taxes on capital gains. Guidelines for cryptocurrency have been issued by the Financial Crimes Enforcement Network (FinCEN). Those who "mine" bitcoins, also known as "miners," are cautioned in the updated guidelines that they are not necessarily immune from legal repercussions. Specifically, the guidelines state that anybody who converts bitcoins into fiat currency may be subject to legal action. It says here:

"A person who creates units of convertible virtual currency and then sells those units to another person for real currency or its equivalent is engaged in transmission to another location and is a money transmitter." "A person who sells those units to another person for real currency or its equivalent."

It would seem that miners are included in this group, which might, in principle, render them subject to MTB classification. Bitcoin miners have expressed their confusion on this matter and have requested more explanation. To this day, this matter has not been discussed openly in a legal proceeding anywhere in the world.

- What is cryptocurrency? Service (Service)

There is a plethora of information and monitoring services pertaining to cryptocurrencies that can be found online. The cryptocurrency market capitalization, price, available supply, and volume can all be seen on CoinMarketcap, which is a good resource for doing so. Reddit is a fantastic platform for users who want to "follow trends" and "stay in touch with the community." There is a wealth of information available on CryptoCoinChart, including a list of cryptocurrencies, information on exchanges, details on arbitrage opportunities, and much more. Our very own website provides a list of crypto currencies along with the daily, weekly, and monthly percentage change in value that each has experienced.

Visitors to Litehack are able to see the network hash rate of a wide variety of cryptocurrencies using one of nine different hashing algorithms. They even offered a graph of the network's hash rate, which allows you to see any trends or indications that the general public's interest in a certain coin is either increasing or decreasing.

A mining guide website that may be found on CoinWarz. This may assist miners in determining which coin will provide the most return on their investment in terms of hash rate, power consumption, and the current market value of the coin when it is exchanged for bitcoin. You are even able to see the current and historical difficulty of each coin.

Indexes Serve As A Convergence Point For Currency Pairs

Indexes have extremely essential roles to play, not only when studying for the use of confluence to confirm price movements, but also when analyzing for other uses of confluence. An index (or gauge) of the value of the United States Dollar is referred to as the U.S. Dollar Index.

When the U.S. dollar acquires "strength" (value), the Index goes up, and when this occurs, we know that all USDXXX pairings begin to likewise gain strength, while the XXX USD pairs begin to decline in value. In contrast, when the Euro gains strength (value), the Index goes down. This is due to the fact that different pairs of currencies have varying degrees of positive and negative correlation with the USD. The same may be said about other couples.

Indexes are used to measure the value of each currency.

1. DXY - Shorthand for the Dollar Index

2. SXY is short for the Swiss Franc Index.

3. BXY, which stands for the British Pound Index

4. JXY -- abbreviation for the Japanese Yen Index

5. AXY, which stands for the Australian Dollar Index

6. ZXY -- This refers to the New Zealand Index

7. CXY, which stands for the Canadian Dollar Index

8. EXY is short for the Euro Index (On trading view, if you search for their abbreviated version, for example JXY, it will come up!)

We have a large number of indexes to keep an eye on for confluence; however, this may be too much for us to handle while trading and may cause a great deal of confusion. At this point, the most prudent thing for us to do is to focus on just one or two of these indexes; for example, I will recommend the DXY, which is the dollar index, and the BXY, which is the British Pound Index. Let's take a look at some instances of how we may utilize these indices to create confluence for trades while also studying the demand and supply of a certain asset. Once you have seen how I have constructed the examples, you are then able to go further in utilising all of the indexes if you so want to do so. However, since I only trade three pairs, I do not use all of the indexes, and there are times when I do not use them at all. You are responsible for determining how well it works for you and developing a trading strategy based on that information; then you will be all set.

EXAMPLE OF A CHART 23 DISPLAYING THE DOLLAR INDEX (DXY) IN RELATION TO VARIOUS CURRENCY PAIRS

We know that this has a positive correlation with the DXY (which means that if the DXY is dropping, the USDCAD will also decrease), but if it was XXXUSD, then we would know that it has a negative correlation (which means that if the DXY is falling, XXXUSD, maybe GBPUSD, would be increasing). The above-mentioned example 23 shows the chart layout with the DXY coming first, followed by the USDCAD.

The use of indexes is not guaranteed to provide accurate results, but they can provide useful information, particularly when the market is getting close to mitigating a zone. As we can see from the example that was given earlier, the DXY and the pair did not mitigate on the same zone; instead, the pair mitigated on a different zone than we had anticipated. Because of this, when I said that the dxy offers a hint, I meant that while the dxy began mitigating a zone, we know that the sale is inevitable, then we should know that we need a supply zone on the currency pair to make us become engaged in the delivery of price, and because we know that the sell is certain, then we should know that we need a supply zone on the currency pair. If you didn't notice the DXY, you could still be waiting for the currency pair to reduce the upper zone, which didn't end up happening. However, the DXY shows that this won't happen.

EXAMPLE OF A CHART THAT DEMONSTRATES THE INFLUENCE OF CURRENCY PAIRS ON THE SWISS FRANC INDEX (XSY)

Simply by glancing at these two charts SXY, which are located above, we already know from which zone the market wants to move from or where a potential mitigation is going to occur. This contrasts with the first illustration, in which the index and the paid have two separate mitigation points. If you can see two mitigation points as in the previous example, then you should make sure that you follow the index since it is the chart that represents the genuine value or price of the currency.

You don't have to use CHFJPY as I have; you may use other pairings instead. whenever you use CADCHF, for example, you'll know that whenever the index indicates a BUY, you should be seeking to SELL because of the negative correlation. Let's have a look at some further instances.

EXAMPLE OF A CHART DEMONSTRATING THE INFLUENCE OF CURRENCY PAIRS ON THE JAPANESE YEN INDEX (JXY) 25.

The following is an illustration of the negative association that I was referring to before. Since there is no pair that corresponds to JPYXXX, we are limited to using XXXJPY as our example currency; hence, we chose USDJPY as our case study currency to compare to the JPY index. Due to the fact that they have a negative correlation with one another, while we are searching for a BUY on the currency pair, we hunt for a SELL on the index, and vice versa, as can be seen in the preceding example. We shall see how the USDJPY will play out later on in this ebook; I have already sent the setup to the mentorship group that I am a part of.

Let us keep an eye out for it.

EXAMPLE OF A CHART THAT DEMONSTRATES THE INFLUENCE OF CURRENCY PAIRS ON THE AUSTRALIA DOLLAR INDEX (AXY)

Repeating the same process over and over again, after conducting your multi-time frame analysis and locating the zone, you can next open the index chart and discover the supply and demand zones that are geographically closest to you and that satisfy the criteria for being referred to as supply and demand zones. Use just a single time frame, such as the H1 or the m30, while analyzing the index since it may be so volatile as a result of market closing hours and gaps. There is no need for multi-time frame analysis on the index.

CHART EXAMPLE 27.

NEW ZEALAND INDEX(ZXY) AS CONFLUENCE WITH CURRENCY PAIRS.

Despite how simple it seems, it requires consistent practice.

The Prospects For The Long-Term Use Of Digital Currencies

The distributed and decentralized nature of a cryptocurrency's network is perhaps the most important aspect to take into consideration while learning about cryptocurrencies. With the expansion of the internet, we may be just'seeing the 'tip of the iceberg' in relation to future innovation, which may leverage undiscovered possibilities for permitting decentralization at a scale that has not been seen or imagined up to this point. Therefore, although in the past there was a need for a vast network, it was only achievable by using a hierarchical structure. As a consequence, there was a need of 'urrendering the power' of that network to a small number of people who had a controlling interest. However, this is no longer necessary. One may argue that Bitcoin symbolizes the decentralization of monetary systems as well as the shift toward more straightforward organizational structures. Bitcoin is an important technological innovation on par with peer-to-peer file sharing and internet telephony (like Skype, for example).

There is very little explicitly produced legal regulation for digital or virtual currency; however, there is a wide range of existing laws that may apply depending on the legal financial framework of the country. These laws include taxation, banking and money transfer regulation, securities regulation, criminal and/or civil law, consumer rights and protection, prison regulation, commodity and stock regulation, and other laws. Therefore, the two most important questions concerning bitcoin are whether or not it can be regarded as a form of legal tender, and whether it can be classified as an asset, whether or not it can be classified as property. It is common practice for nations to explicitly define money as the legal tender of another nation (for example, the US dollar), which prevents such nations from recognizing other 'currencies' as technically a currency. Germany is a noteworthy exception to this rule since it allows for the idea of a 'unit of account,' which may thus be used as a kind of 'private money,' and it can be used in'multilateral clearing circle,' respectively. To look at it from the opposite perspective, if it were to be considered property, the most obvious difference would be that, unlike property, digital currencies may be divided up into much smaller amounts. This is not the case with property. Digital currencies are often accepted in developed economies because of their open financial systems. The United States of America has been given the most advice and has a significant presence on the map below. Economies that are governed by capital are considered to be either contentious or hospitable by definition. The question has not yet been answered for several countries in Africa and a few other places across the world.

Beginning with the fundamentals of democratic participation, it is immediately obvious that bitcoin does not qualify for the positive social impact component of such an aim. This is due to the fact that bitcoin's value is not one it can exert influence on, but rather is subject to the forces of the market. Nevertheless, any "new" crypto-currency would be able to provide democratic participation if the virtual currency has different norms of administration and issuance based on democratic values that are more commonly accepted in society.

So what if a "digital" currency could provide a valid alternative to existing forms of money in performing the role of contributing positively to: the goal of promoting a socially inclusive culture, the equanimity of opportunity, and the promotion of mutualism; all of which, as their very names imply, are alternatives and/or complementary to an official or national sovereign currency? Although they are still in their infancy, the rate of innovation in the field of cryptocurrencies has been dramatic. Virtual cryptocurrencies like as bitcoin represent a new and emerging dynamic in the system.

The 'effectiveness' of money to bring about positive social and environmental change is determined by a number of factors, including pervasive political ideology, the economic environment, the desire of local communities and individuals to pursue alternative social outcomes while also seeking to maximize economic opportunity, the building of social capital, and many other factors. If a local digital currency could be created with the intention of injecting more resilience into a local economy and improving economic results, then the introduction of a more widespread form of the currency would merit examination. When the existing economic system fails to provide, it may be seen in a variety of ways, some of which include increased social isolation, higher crime rates, physical dereliction, poor health, and a lack of a sense of community, amongst other unfavorable effects on society.

On The Way To Accumulating Millions Of Dollars

Mining cryptocurrencies and trading them on exchanges are the two most lucrative ways to generate money with them. You can theoretically never stop making money if you keep mining for Bitcoins, provided that the various business sectors continue to be active. However, despite all of the difficulties involved, mining Bitcoins has become a very risky endeavor in recent years. Converting your personal computer into an excavator will most likely cause it to become noisy and heated up. To mine even a single Bitcoin would call for a significant financial commitment on your part. A more powerful computer might have been purchased with the time and money that was wasted.

Conduct research on various forms of cryptocurrency.

Nonetheless, in the event that you approach some real processing influence and you do not need to pay the bills, you may benefit from this situation.

The most practical approach to earning a million dollars with Bitcoins will be to trade them via the most prominent exchanges, such as Coinbase. Back in 2011, one bitcoin could be acquired for a total of ten dollars. In essence, you should have acquired around one thousand Bitcoins back when they were selling at a discount. If you had done this in 2011, it would have cost you around $10,000, which would make you a billionaire today.

There is a good chance that you may earn a million dollars using Bitcoins right now, but you will need some starting cash. The price of bitcoins may move by a number of percentage points on a daily basis (on May 22, 2017, the price rose by 10%). Bitcoin trades conducted throughout the day will be fraught with risk; but, where there is volatility, opportunity may be found. A plan with a longer time horizon must be adopted and the business must be shut down if this is not the case, regardless of whether or not you believed Bitcoins would be successful. If you believe that one day organizations, advertising makers, and online merchants will accept Bitcoin as a form of payment, you may want to consider going long on the cryptocurrency. The value diagram is screaming "bubble," yet your purpose of passage relies on you making a purchase at this time despite the fact that it would be inconceivably risky to do so. However, you should try not to expect to observe a rapid growth in the company right now.

On the other hand, in the case that you have a strong confidence that Bitcoin will ultimately fail, you should short the digital currency in any way that you can. This would still be a very risky endeavor, but if the Bitcoin market is genuinely doomed to fail, then why not try to become wealthy when the air bubble bursts? To "short" a Bitcoin, you will either need to be creative or join a trade that allows you to do so. Either way, you will need to do one of two things.

The Bitcoin protocol has been tested and validated, and it is very close to becoming the industry standard. It is still considered an excellent prospect for financial speculation. If you are anything like me, you probably passed up the opportunity to invest in Bitcoins when the price was far lower than it is now. However, it is feasible that one may still invest in Bitcoins at this moment in time. The point at which this is possible may not have passed yet. Even while the price of a single Bitcoin now stands at over $3,400, there is a possibility that this figure may drastically rise as the currency continues to gain widespread acceptance. Keep in mind that a Bitcoin may be divided up to the eighth decimal place, and that as time goes on, it will become an order of magnitude more expensive to mine.

It also benefits from the snowball effect and the organizer effect, both of which serve to foster its development. There is no reason why a single Bitcoin cannot end up being significantly justified regardless of a million dollars in principle, and countless other people believe that it most likely will in the end.

The Ether is frequently referred to, as the global computer since it can perform any logical step of a computational process. Ethereum is a decentralized application platform that has its own Bitcoin counterpart cryptocurrency. Bitcoin, on the other hand, is a decentralized money solely. This capability opens up a wide variety of doors for potential applications.

VitalikButerin, who came up with the idea for Ethereum a few years ago, was just twenty-two years old at the time. At the time, he was hailed as bright and the "Einstein of blockchain technology."

Backers contributed more than $18 million to the Ethereum project at the time, propelling it to the position of the fourth biggest crowd-funded project of all time. This combination of Ethereum's decentralized cryptographic architecture and Turing fulfillment might make it possible to implement purposes that have not been considered before.

It is anticipated that the price of Ether would rise far more quickly than that of Bitcoin. This is due to the fact that while they are still in their infancy, there are already operating decentralized apps that are governed by Ethereum's (Ether) coin. This is the case despite the fact that they are still in their infancy.

In addition, Ethereum has introduced the concept of what is known as a "Smart contract," which is a contract that is written in code and activated when it is deposited on the Ethereumblockchain. It's possible for an agreement to change hands between retailers depending on the

69

circumstances. Taking into account applications like as decentralized escrow, rental contracts, and property deeds is taken into account here.

You should supply your subscribers with weekly and monthly market updates and share the specifics of your bitcoin portfolio with them. Maintain an up-to-date awareness of all news pertaining to digital currencies; do research into several initial coin offerings; and make opportunities available to backers as they become available. Over the course of the preceding year, we were able to amass a fortune in various types of digital currency, and a few of our backers have shared their experiences, including the fact that they were able to retire early due to their early involvement with various forms of cryptographic currency.

There is currently only a very tiny percentage of the world's population that is familiar with the idea of blockchain technology or even has any bitcoin, which is a reality that presents a significant opportunity for those who choose to use this digital monetary technology. That will change as more individuals become aware of the many forms of returns that are being made by investing in these digital currencies. This will cause the situation to reverse.

If you are new to investing in cryptocurrencies, it is highly essential to make sure that you educate yourself on the risks involved before you begin to transfer or receive any significant amounts of money. This should be done before you invest any significant amount of money. When compared to just purchasing stocks with your money market fund, this strategy unquestionably calls for a greater financial commitment as well as a higher level of patience; nevertheless, the rewards more than justify the extra work.

A great deal of enthusiasm may be attributed to the possibilities presented by blockchain technology as well as the rewards on investment offered by cryptocurrencies. It is genuinely groundbreaking technology that is anticipated to have a substantial impact on a number of different businesses that are worth several billions of dollars each. Those that get in on the ground floor early have a real shot at a once-in-a-lifetime chance to amass a fortune.

It is quite possible that this is the only piece of financial news that covers precious metals and digital currencies in this level of depth. They are both superior than bank-issued fiat money paper notes, and the value of both of them continues to rise, whilst the value of one dollar continues to decrease in comparison to other currencies.

The sudden growth in popularity of Ethereum has brought cryptocurrency and blockchain technology back into the mainstream media spotlight. The promise that those who have the computers and the knowledge to undertake mining may bring home large payoffs in a Bitcoin-like race to riches and capture as much of this virtual money as they possibly can has caused the price of graphics cards to skyrocket. Regardless of this fact, how easy is it to amass a fortune via the trade of digital currency? Also, would it be beneficial to start now rather than later?

Determine What Your Risk Is.

Defining your risk at each and every chance that presents itself is essential if you want your trading career to be successful. This involves reducing the size of your trade, taking profits when there is significant resistance, or even waiting for a more favorable entry point before scaling in. Your ability to actively and properly define your risk will have significant repercussions on the overall health of your bankroll over the long run.

Your refusal to sell at a loss is a truly harmful habit, and you should get rid of it as soon as possible. I have firsthandexperience, therefore I am aware of how difficult it is to kick this habit, as well as how severe the consequences may be for engaging in it. In a nutshell, you need to get rid of your losing trades before they wipe out your whole trading account.

"Every single devastating loss you are forced to take was once a minor loss that you refused to accept."

As a trader, I can't tell you how many times I turned down a minor loss in order to hold onto a position, only to have that decision backfire on me later. When I checked my brokerage account, finding that position in red made me feel uneasy, and as a result, I was hesitant to sell off any of my holdings because of it. Because selling would have locked up the loss indefinitely, I decided to keep holding out hope that I can turn things around. After that, what happened? That very little loss ballooned into a significant one.

I refused to sell or take my medication because I was so obstinate, and as a result, I stood there paralyzed in fear.

"By refusing to take even a modest loss, one can frequently find themselves in a position where they can refuse to take a significant loss."

What steps can you take to ensure that you do not get trapped in this situation? Create a trading strategy and adhere to it, which naturally involves utilizing a stop loss based on the invalidation of your trading thesis. This should be your first step in the trading process.

Once your trade is sufficiently profitable, you should adjust your stop loss such that it either meets or exceeds your break-even point. The tension and worry that comes with maintaining a posture may be alleviated to a great extent by using this strategy. Because I want to start "free riding" as quickly as possible, I find that this method works very well for me. You may argue that I am probably missing out on some benefits, but I am happy with that since I prefer to define the level of risk I am willing to take. In addition to that, this helps define how stressed I am.

"Converting your stop-loss order into a take-profit order is an excellent strategy for lowering your overall stress level."

Standards for Non-Ethereum-Based Non-Fungible Tokens

When it comes to the generation of non-fungible tokens, the Ethereum network is presently the platform that is both the most developed and the most user-friendly option available. This is due to the fact that it was designed specifically for this purpose. However, other available networks create their own versions of an NFT using standards that are not based on Ethereum. Let's investigate some of the various networks that are available.

items of value

On the blockchain, dGoods is an open-source and cost-free standard that ensures ownership and liquidity of digital goods and assets. Cross-chain capabilities are provided by the platform, which enable interoperability between two separate blockchains. The uniform construction of the many blockchains makes it possible for them to connect with one another via the use of a technology known as cross-chain communication. At present time, the platform only supports cross-chain functionality between two distinct blockchains, namely EOS and Microsoft

Azure; however, there are future expansion plans to include cross-chain functionality between more blockchains. NFTs that were generated using the dGoods standard will, despite this, be able to interact across the blockchains of EOS and Microsoft Azure for the time being.

The COSMOS

To describe that the platform is an ecosystem of numerous blockchains is another way of referring to the decentralized network of independent parallel blockchains that make up Cosmos. The platform is essentially an Internet of Blockchains that are meant to connect with one another in a manner that is decentralized. Therefore, exactly like dGoods, the blockchains that are managed by the Cosmos platform are capable of interacting with one another.

Because it makes use of a collection of open-source technologies including Tendermint, The Cosmos Software Development Kit (SDK), and IBC, the platform is in a position to realize the interoperability across the platforms. People are able to construct blockchain applications that are unique to their needs, secure, scalable, and interoperable by using these open-source tools.

The development team for the platform is now working on a standalone NFT module that will be spliced into the Cosmos software development kit (SDK). As a result, non-fungible tokens (NFTs) developed using the Cosmos Standard will be able to freely interact with numerous blockchains.

FLOW

The Flow blockchain is a relatively new distributed ledger system that was developed to run next-generation apps, games, and other types of digital assets. Cadence is a brand new programming language that was developed by the group that was responsible for the invention of the CryptoKitties game. Cadence was implemented on the Flow network. The NFTs are converted into resources that users may keep in their accounts thanks to this piece of code. Cadence programming includes a number of significant ownership guidelines, all of which are rigorously policed by the platform. Because of the constraints that govern the programming, non-fungible tokens (NFTs) made in accordance with the Cadence standard have only one owner, and they cannot be lost, replicated, or deleted by mistake or on purpose. The basis of these regulations is that they serve as safeguards that enable owners to feel secure in the knowledge that their NFTs are safe and represented as a digital asset that holds genuine worth. This is made possible by the fact that these rules function as protections that allow owners to know that their NFTs are safe.

Ethereum (ETH)

Because of the way that the internet is organized today, all of your sensitive data, including financial information, personal data, and even passwords, are kept on a cloud server that is jointly controlled by many businesses.

Facebook has a server, just like Amazon and PayPal do, and even your neighborhood community financial institution likely has a database where it stores all of the personal information of its users.

The management of these databases is handled by a group of experts who have been entrusted with the management and security of the data, as well as the reduction of the expenses associated with hosting and uptime.

However, doing so leaves your data vulnerable to attack by cybercriminals and other unauthorized parties since they are able to acquire access to your information by hacking into the servers of the organizations that store it.

This is referred regarded as the "Original Sin of the Internet" by Brain Behlendorf, the person who developed the Apache Web Server.

Many individuals, like Behlendorf, are of the opinion that the Internet ought to be decentralized in such a manner that users may still keep their privacy even while using the service.

Therefore, in the same way that bitcoin and other alternative cryptocurrencies were developed in order to decentralize the conventional monetary system, ethereum was developed in order to make use of blockchain technology in order to decentralize the storage and transmission of data on the internet.

The necessity for centralized servers and clouds is reduced thanks to Ethereum, which replaces them with a network of "nodes" that are operated by volunteers located in different parts of the globe.

When you visit a typical app store, you'll find a wide selection of applications that you can download and use on your smartphone. However, many apps depend on third parties (such as Google or Apple) to help store your personal data, credit card information, or shopping history.

These third parties are in charge of deciding the categories of applications that are available for you to download into your computer.

Ethereum is working toward giving back the custody of this data as well as the creative rights associated with programs to their original developers.

Because of the ability of developers to create decentralized applications, a single organization would no longer have control over the programs that are used.

Ethereum functions much like a decentralized app store, allowing anybody to publish their own applications without the need for a third party to handle the information or functionality of the user's account.

It will be possible for users and providers to connect directly with one another.

Chapter Seven: Legalities, Risks, and Predictions for Cryptocurrency

Regarding the law

Different nations have different policies when it comes to whether or not cryptocurrencies are legal. The use of cryptocurrencies is a relatively recent development. As a result of the fact that many nations' governments are currently grappling with the challenge of making sense of this novel occurrence, little progress has been made toward the establishment of legal frameworks to govern its use. A number of nations, most notably Bitcoin, have made cryptocurrency transactions valid forms of money. Some people consider cryptocurrencies to be a legitimate asset. Since cryptocurrencies do not have a clear definition in certain nations' legal systems, this leaves them in a gray area where they are neither legal nor unlawful. However, other nations have decided to label it as unlawful and have placed an outright prohibition on its consumption.

Cryptocurrencies are recognized as convertible, decentralized money that may be used as a means of exchange, a store of value, and a unit of account in the United States. Additionally, cryptocurrencies can be mined to create additional units of cryptocurrency. However, they have not been specifically designated as currency by the relevant authorities. Bitcoin and other cryptocurrencies are subject to the same taxes as any other asset that is kept for the purpose of investing. The Financial Crimes Enforcement Network of the United States (FinCEN) has produced rules that categorize cryptocurrency exchanges as Money Transmitting Businesses (MTBs). This classification compels cryptocurrency exchanges to implement Know Your Client (KYC) and Anti-Money Laundering (AML) procedures. The Commodity Futures Trading Commission (CFTC) and the Securities and Exchange Commission (SEC) of the United States have not yet devised any regulations regarding the use of cryptocurrencies. The usage of cryptocurrencies is regulated in a manner that varies significantly amongst the states that make up the United States.

In a similar vein, the legal frameworks of other nations take a variety of approaches to the usage of cryptocurrencies. The use of cryptocurrencies as a form of legal money is not now possible in Canada. Nevertheless, users are expected to pay taxes in the same manner as they do for speculative purchases. Because cryptocurrency exchanges are not considered to be MTBs in Canada, the Canadian government does not hold them accountable for the implementation of anti-laundering procedures. Cryptocurrencies are not yet recognized as a form of legal money in Australia; hence, they are not subject to taxation. However, the government is considering imposing a tax on cryptocurrency transactions. Bitcoin has been given formal status as a form of legal money in Japan. The Chinese government does not allow banks or other financial organizations to utilize cryptocurrencies like bitcoin or ethereum as a form of legal tender. Individuals are still free to trade cryptocurrencies according to their own whims. The government of Russia has implemented regulations that prohibit the usage of virtual currencies.

The majority of the European Union does not regulate virtual currencies in any meaningful way. In certain nations, such as France, there are no explicit rules that control the use of virtual currencies, while Germany considers them to be foreign currencies. In a similar vein, Spain does not have any governmental standards to govern the usage of virtual currencies. Despite this, cryptocurrencies are nevertheless subject to taxation in accordance with the guidelines for bartering. The use of cryptocurrencies is neither regulated nor recognized as a form of currency in Turkey. The Israeli government is continuing doing research on digital currencies, with the intention of beginning to tax them in the near future.

Counterparty, often known as XCP

Contrary to popular belief, Counterparty is not, in and of itself, a cryptocurrency. It does have a token called XCP that can be purchased, sold, or traded, but these functions are really a side effect of Counterparty's primary goal, which is to facilitate peer-to-peer cryptocurrency transactions. Counterparty is a platform that is built on Bitcoin that allows for the creation of additional currencies and other assets on top of the blockchain that Bitcoin uses. Although they are not Bitcoins in and of themselves, the transaction mechanism for them is the same. They may also be used in combination with normal Bitcoin addresses, which makes bookkeeping more straightforward for Bitcoin users. Despite the fact that these resources are shared, the balances in one's Counterparty wallet and Bitcoin wallet are completely separate from one another.

At the peak of its popularity, there were dozens, if not hundreds, of different tokens that were based on the Counterparty platform. There were tokens that represented video game assets, IOUs for digital and real items, voting rights in enterprises and organizations, access to members-only sections of websites, and a lot of other things like that.

The blockchain platform Counterparty was first used in the construction of SCJX, which was STORJ's forerunner and was detailed before. LTBcoin is an example of a currency that was produced by Counterparty but is not as well known as some of the other examples. It was launched by the creators of the Let's Talk Bitcoin podcast, which is a prominent Bitcoin podcast. They provide the cash as a token of appreciation to those who have assisted them in producing the podcast in one way or another. When a customer pays with LTBcoin, they are entitled to a significant discount not just for podcast services but also for a variety of online retailers with whom LTB has collaborated. In addition to that, it may be used as a tip. It's a great illustration of a cryptocurrency that's designed just for a limited audience of users.

counterparty.io is the domain name of Counterparty's main website.

Used For The Purpose Of Accumulating Wealth

When there are high levels of inflation in the country's fiat currency, Bitcoin may be a useful alternative. Historically, people have turned to Bitcoin at times of severe economic distress. Gold operates in the same manner. If Bitcoin is going to be taken seriously as a potential store of value or wealth, it has to satisfy two conditions.

It should not be anything that spoils easily.

The value does not rise with passage of time.

The second criterion, on the other hand, may be dated. Bitcoin may be worth less in the future, according to the opinions of some naysayers, if a newer and more advanced technology is developed. Bitcoin, on the other hand, has already reached a certain market threshold where the concept itself has inherent worth, similar to an email address or an account you have with a social networking platform. If you are not the only one having an email account, then the usage of email is not as beneficial as it would otherwise be. On the other hand, the more people who use a piece of technology, the simpler it becomes and the more useful it is.

Gold has historically been used as a contingency plan or "hedge" against the performance of various financial markets. Gold prices have a tendency to rise during times of war or financial crisis, which coincide with fast falls throughout global markets. Recent events, however, have not followed this pattern. Gold prices have remained relatively unchanged, but those of bitcoin have almost quadrupled over the last year. Bitcoin's development and appeal have been bolstered by the unpredictability of the current state of the global financial system.

Wallets made of paper

paper wallets private information that is written down on paper and stored in a paper wallet. When coins are sent electronically, they often feature QR codes that the sender may scan.

Advantages Cost-effectiveness

Because private keys are not digitally saved, they are safe from both cybercriminals and malfunctions in the underlying hardware.

Cons

prone to mistakes made by humans

Paper is susceptible to damage and deterioration in particular settings due to its fragility.

It is not practical for use in regular business dealings.

You are able to generate unprotected paper wallets online by using many sources. However, it is important to keep in mind that these websites link to the internet, which makes them insecure. In the event that the website is hacked, the perpetrators will have access to your information and will be able to steal the private key that you generated.

Wallets Made of Hardware

Hardware wallets are literal storage devices that may be carried about with you and hold your private key. The majority of these hardware wallets are encrypted flash drive sticks, and they are the most frequent kind. These are quite similar to the ones that you manufacture; the only difference is that someone else is responsible for establishing the safety measures. People who are not comfortable with technology will profit from this. The majority of these hardware wallets come with backup software already installed in case you misplace your keys.

In order to guarantee that no one other than the wallet's owner may access the stored data, hardware wallets call for a method known as two-factor authentication, or 2FA. A physical flash drive stick that you connect into your computer is one example of a factor. Another factor is a four-digit PIN number, which is analogous to the PIN that you use when withdrawing money from an ATM card.

Pros

To be hacked with difficulty

Because of the two-factor authentication (2FA), your digital wallet will continue to be inaccessible even if malware or a virus infects your computer.

Your device is the only place where the private key will ever be stored; your computer will never have access to it.

You are free to take the flash drive with you wherever you go.

When compared to paper wallets, digital wallets make transactions more simpler.

When you wish to establish numerous Bitcoin accounts, it is advantageous that you can store many addresses on a single device since it allows you to do so.

They are more stylish than any folded piece of paper could ever be Pros

More expensive than traditional paper wallets

prone to problems with the hardware, deterioration, and advancements in technology

Several distinct cryptocurrencies may be stored in a variety of wallets.

It is impossible to have faith that the supplier would supply a wallet that has not been used. A wallet that has been used before is a major security risk. You should only purchase from authorized retailers.

Ledger and Trezor are now the two most popular hardware wallets. In addition to portability and safety, each of them also offers a straightforward and uncomplicated user experience.

An Explanation Of The Technology Behind The Blockchain

A number of changes have taken place in the structure of the global financial system.

When people wanted to acquire anything in the past, about three hundred years ago, they were forced to depend on barter trading. This required them to bring an item that they already had, and then they had to find someone who needed what they already possessed and had what they needed to provide.

For instance, if you were in need of some green vegetables but also had some sweet potatoes, you would have to find someone else who was in the same position as you with regard to both the green vegetables and the sweet potatoes.

If they had vegetables but did not have a need for sweet potatoes, then it was impossible for them to engage in a transaction. This was the kind of convoluted financial structure that the whole globe relied on for a number of years.

As a result, a different system was developed; fiat currency was established so that people could use them to purchase and sell without having to go through the stress of finding someone to trade their goods for money.

However, before long, even fiat money was no longer sufficient because of the development of the internet, which turned the globe into a global village and allowed individuals from various nations and continents to do business with one another. As a result of the introduction of payment solutions such as credit cards, PayPal, and other payment solutions that enabled people to transact with whoever they wanted, making payments to business acquaintances located on different continents was no longer a challenge. However, remote payments were difficult due to the fact that international wire transfers were both complicated and expensive.

However, each and every one of the banking and payment systems that were available at the time was plagued with a few issues.

Interference from the Government: The government is in charge of the creation of traditional fiat money, as well as its regulation and control, and every choice the government takes has the potential to influence the wealth of anybody who keeps their wealth denominated in that currency.

For example, if a country's government chooses to lower the value of its currency, the people living in that nation would see a reduction in the value of their wealth as well as any investments and savings they may have.

Interference from a Third Party: In order for transactions to be completed using fiat cash, there is a need for the involvement of a third party. For example, if your buddy Fred needs to transfer you some money, he will need to do it via his bank, and you will also need the confirmation of the transaction from your bank.

Because individuals do not trust one another, there is always a need for a financial institution to facilitate, witness, and validate financial transactions. This third party involvement is necessary because of the lack of trust that exists between people.

Another disadvantage of using fiat cash is that there is no guarantee of personal privacy. You are required to provide the bank with a variety of personal and professional facts, including your name, address, social security number, and job information, before you may create an account with the bank or do business using fiat money.

Even if doing this is vital for preventing money laundering and for the sake of tax legislation, the reality that you cannot have privacy when doing business with conventional fiat currency or financial institutions does not alter regardless of whether or not you do this.

Costs Involved in Transactions: Although the expenses of doing business locally may be low, it's a whole other ballgame when you have to conduct business on a global scale.

If you are a businessperson who is required to conduct a significant number of foreign transactions, you would welcome a financial system that enables you to do business on a global scale at a fraction of the typical cost. Typically, the transaction costs associated with overseas transactions are relatively high.

Theft Have you ever had your credit card information stolen or had someone get into your bank account? These are some of the difficulties that come with using conventional financial systems, such as the fact that your money might be lost as a result of the bank's actions or inactions.

Therefore, a person or group of people working under the moniker 'Satoshi Nakamoto' set to work to establish a financial system that aims to overcome the majority of the issues described in the paragraphs above.

They were successful in developing the blockchain technology, which allowed them to establish the world's first cryptocurrency, known as Bitcoin.

The Finest Bitcoin Trading Platforms Available Today

The following is a list of the most reliable platforms for trading Bitcoin based on research.

Plus500 on Coinbase.com.

AvaTradeeToro IG XTB and XTB are all options.

Market's Dot Com

The website Trade.com

A few of the brokers are Admiral Markets, UFX, and Ayrex.

HOW IS ONLINE CURRENCY SUCH AS BITCOIN DIFFERENT FROM PAPER CURRENCY?

Bitcoin is a decentralized digital currency. It does not exist in the same type of physical form as the currency and coin that we are accustomed to seeing. Even in the shape of physical Monopoly money, you won't be able to find it. It is electrons, not molecules, that are involved here. But you should also think about how much cash you personally deal with. You get a paycheck, which you then either bring to the bank or have automatically deposited there, in which case you do not even have to look at the paper it is not written on. After that, you may access the funds with a debit card (or a checkbook, if you choose). When you win, you get 10% of the pot in the form of cash, which you may keep in your wallet or purse. It seems that almost ninety percent of the funds that you handle are only electronic representations stored in a spreadsheet or database.

Volatility (lat.)

It can seem that Bitcoin's price is too unpredictable and that it fluctuates erratically like crazy.

Compared to the US Dollar, the Euro, and the British Pound, the yuan is a lot more stable. It is also far more stable when compared to the currency of Ukraine,

Argentina, and dozens of other currencies.

The deflationary effects of value Bitcoin

This indicates that there is a finite amount available, and no one can just print more of it.

There was a day in the former Soviet Union when the authorities made the decision to cut the value of the country's official currency by a factor of 10. That is not something that can be done with bitcoin.

Western Union and other services that are comparable often charge transaction fees ranging from 1% to 5% of the amount being transferred. The typical charge for making a transaction with Bitcoin is only a few of cents, and if you're not in a rush, you may even pay less than that.

Ability to be moved easily

As long as you are able to tear 256 bits, you are able to have Bitcoin (this is something that 99% all computers are able to achieve). You have the option of writing the key down on the piece of paper or just remembering it.

Transportation capability

The typical duration of a transaction is quite brief (one second). If, on the other hand, your transaction is of the utmost significance, you will be required to wait for six blocks, or six confirmations, which will typically take around an hour.

Assurance of safety

There are no other options available to you except the FDIC insurance in the event that your bank fails. If you don't have the key, there aren't many things that can go wrong with Bitcoin.

denial of ability

There is one single point of failure at the bank. If your financial institution fails, it will fail catastrophically. The decentralized and open-source structure of Bitcoin renders it vulnerable to a wide variety of various kinds of attacks. In order to effectively infect millions of computers or points of access simultaneously, a hacker or group of hackers will need to successfully infect millions of machines simultaneously.

Ability to be divided:

You are able to possess/buy/transfer a little amount of 0.0000071411 USD worth of Bitcoin (at the current price). It is the smallest unit possible, and one t is equivalent to 0.00000001 BTC.

A Quick Note Regarding Blockchain

To put it in the simplest words possible, a blockchain is a digital ledger of transactions. This is not unlike to the ledgers that have been used by humans for hundreds of years to record sales and purchases. In point of fact, the role of a digital ledger is very much equivalent to that of a traditional ledger in that it records debts and credits owed and received by various individuals. This is the fundamental idea that underpins blockchain technology; the difference is in who controls the ledger and who verifies the transactions.

Blockchains function in a fundamentally different way in one important respect: they are completely decentralized. There is neither a central clearing house like a bank, nor is there a central ledger kept by a single organization or individual. Instead, the ledger is distributed throughout a vast network of computers that are referred to as nodes. These nodes each have a copy of the whole ledger stored on their own hard drives, and together they form the ledger. These nodes are linked to one another using a piece of software known as a peer-to-peer (P2P) client. This piece of software synchronizes data throughout the network of nodes and ensures that everyone has access to the same version of the ledger at all times.

When a new transaction is added to a blockchain, it is first encrypted using technology that is considered to be state-of-the-art in the field of cryptography. After being encrypted, the transaction is then converted into something that is called a block. A block is essentially the word that is used to refer to a group of newly encrypted transactions. This block is then broadcast (or transmitted) to the network of computer nodes, where it is validated by the node. Once verified, the block is sent on via the network so that it may be appended to the end of the ledger on everyone's computer, under the list of all the blocks that have come before it. This is referred to as the chain, which is why the technology is sometimes called a blockchain.The transaction may be considered finished after it has been sanctioned and entered into the ledger. The operation of cryptocurrencies such as Bitcoin may be explained like this.

Before being added to the ledger, all transactions (or blocks) on a blockchain are checked for accuracy by the nodes that make up the network. This ensures that there is no single point of failure and no single approval channel for transactions. If a hacker wanted to effectively tamper with the ledger on a blockchain, they would need to simultaneously hack a milllion of machines, which is not impossible. However, it would take a great deal of effort. A hacker would also be very much unable of bringing down a blockchain network because, once again, they would need to be able to shut down each and every computer that is part of a network of computers that are distributed all over the world.

The method of encryption, in and of itself, is also an important consideration. Blockchains, such as the one used by Bitcoin, use techniques that are purposefully difficult for the sake of their verification procedure. In the case of Bitcoin, blocks are confirmed by nodes carrying out a purposefully labor- and time-intensive set of computations. These computations often take the shape of riddles or complex mathematical problems, which means that verification is neither immediate nor easily accessible. Nodes who provide resources to the verification of blocks are rewarded with a transaction fee and a bounty of newly-minted Bitcoins. These nodes also get credit for their contributions. The purpose of these is twofold: first, they incentivize users to participate in the network as nodes (mining new currency units needs relatively powerful computers and a significant amount of electricity), and second, they manage the process of creating new currency units, also known as minting. The process of developing a brand-new commodity requires a substantial investment of time and energy (on the part of a computer, in this particular instance), and hence, this practice is known as mining. It also indicates that the most independent method possible is used to verify financial transactions. This method is more independent than a government-regulated organization such as the FSA.

Because blockchains are decentralized, democratic, and highly secure, they can function without the requirement for external regulation (because they are capable of self-regulation) or oversight from the government or any other opaque institution. ancillary to the primary topic. They are successful not in spite of the fact that people don't trust one another but rather because of it.

Types OfNfts

Because the definition of what makes a non-financial transaction (NFT) is still relatively vague, almost anything may be categorized as an NFT. This is because of the ambiguity around the notion. The following is a list of the non-fiction books that are now available on the market that are considered to be the most reasonable and broad.

Gaining An Understanding Of The Varieties Of Transactions That Are Not Financial

In recent years, there has been a significant uptick in interest about the creation of one-of-a-kind digital assets by using blockchain technology. Non-fungible tokens, more often referred to as NFTs, are notable topics that will get a large amount of attention in the year 2021. As a direct result of this, there has been a discernible rise in the number of people interested in gaining a deeper understanding of the many types of nonlinear optical fibers.

People are interested in non-traditional financial instruments (NFTs) because they provide the possibility of economically attractive opportunities, but they are also interested in the idea of existing asset management practices being disrupted. The steady growth of non-fungible tokens is likely to result in a multitude of investment and development opportunities for non-fungible tokens (NFTs). As a consequence of this, having a solid grasp of the different types of non-fungible tickets can aid you in making more informed decisions as you go along your NFT journey.

Art

 The kind of non-fiction storytelling most often used is one that involves creative expression. As a result of the development of NFTs, artists now have a fantastic opportunity to sell their finest works online in the same manner in which they would sell them in a traditional retail establishment. At the present, many of the nonlinear optical transducers that are the most expensive are also works of art. According to Luno, the well-known artist Beeple's "EVERYDAY'S: THE FIRST 5000 DAYS" is the NFT with the highest value that has ever been sold, making it the most costly NFT that has ever been sold. An astounding sixty-nine million dollars was paid for this piece of artwork. In addition to this, there are non-financial transactions (NFTs) that are very expensive and are wreaking havoc on the bank accounts of billionaires.

This is also true for works of art created using video. Short films and even animated GIFs with a sense of humor have been bringing in millions of dollars and selling like hotcakes. The ten-second looping video titled "Crossroad," which portrays a naked Donald Trump laid out on the ground, sold for a record-breaking price of $6.6 million, making it the most expensive video item that has ever been sold on eBay. Beeple is responsible for the creation of this one as well.

The NFT spectrum also has a significant emphasis on music as a significant component. Since the beginning of recorded history, music has been created and distributed on a wide variety of formats, such as phonograph records, audio cassettes, compact discs, and, more recently, digitally via the use of the internet. On the other side, NFTs have recently gained increased popularity among DJs and musicians, which has led to some of these individuals earning millions of dollars in a very short period of time.

Most of the time, musicians are only paid a portion of the money that their work brings in since streaming services and record companies have reduced the amount of money they pay artists. Because artists have the potential to keep close to one hundred percent of the money made via non-financial transactions, a growing number of musicians are opting to conduct business in this manner.

Items from Video Games

The field of NFT has seen the arrival of a new frontier with the advent of video games. Tokens that are non-transferable are not being sold by companies as complete games. They will, however, be selling in-game content such as characters, skins, and several other items. Users now have the ability to acquire millions of copies of downloadable content items. On the other hand, an NFT item will be one of a kind and will only be available to a certain purchaser. The NFT marketplace makes it possible for developers to offer regular downloadable content (DLC), while also allowing them to sell a limited edition version of the same DLC.

Collectible Playing Cards and Other Items

There are several ways in which non-fungible tokens (NFTs) might be likened to digital trading cards. The non-fantasy trading card market is not an exception to the rule that limited edition baseball cards may fetch prices in the hundreds of dollars. This is common information. On the market, it is possible to buy and trade digital copies of trading cards, and these copies may be stored and displayed in the same manner as real trading cards can be supported. In addition, much like the originals, some of these copies sell for more than one million dollars.

On the NFT market, businesses have the ability to offer a wide variety of collecting items in addition to traditional trading cards. If something is regarded to be collectable, then it is possible to trade it or sell it on the open market.

Significant Events in Sports

A recall of amazing athletic events is what non-fantasy trading cards (NFTs) provide, which is something that cannot be recreated in the real world. These are short films that highlight significant moments in sports that are definitely worth seeing, such as slam dunks that changed the game or touchdowns that changed the game. Even though some of these recordings are just 10 seconds long, they may sell for more than $200,000 if they are in good condition.

Memes (n.)

If you were under the impression that the internet couldn't get any more fun, you'll be pleased to know that the NFT market now enables buyers and sellers to trade memes. One thing that sets this meme apart from others is that in certain instances, the person who is shown in it is also the one who is selling the item. Earnings per meme range from $30,000 to $770,000, and many of the internet's most famous memes, such as "Nyan Cat," "Bad Luck Brian," "Disaster Girl," and others, are included on this list. At a recent auction, the Doge meme, which is considered to be the most expensive meme ever, was sold for a staggering $4 million.

Domain Names (or DNs)

The NFT fever has spread to domain names, which are vulnerable to the sickness now that it has spread. It is possible to register a domain name and subsequently sell it on the NFT market, and there are various benefits to choosing this path rather than one of the other available choices. It is common practice to be forced to pay a fee to a third-party company in order to have your occupational title administered. If you acquire one on the NFT market, you will be able to claim exclusive ownership of the word, which will remove the need for a third party to act as a middleman in the transaction.

Online Clothing Stores

Why should the fashion industry be any different from the rest of the NFT sector, which does all of its buying and selling electronically? You could spend a lot of money on a fantastic bikini, but you won't be able to wear it the way it was intended to be worn. Those who invest in fashion NFTs will do the dressing of their virtual avatars rather than their actual avatars in real life.

This may seem absurd, but bear in mind that someone, somewhere in the globe, paid up $4 million in order to acquire ownership to the Doge meme. Those who are more extravagant and on the cutting edge of fashion are the ones who get to be the proud owners of virtual purses and jewels. These will all, without a doubt, be one-of-a-kind masterpieces, and there will only be a select number available.

Various Goods Available Via the Internet

The other components on this list were simple to explain, but the NFT market is like the wild west of internet commerce, as seen by the crisis that happened in the NFT market a few months ago. Other items on this list were basic to express.

As was previously said, Jack Dorsey basically transacted the sale of a single tweet. Because of this, anybody is now able to sell whatever they want on the NFT market, which is exactly what the market is intended to be used for. When it comes to the kinds of things that people may sell on the internet, there is no limit to the kinds of things that people can sell. People can sell tweets, Facebook status updates, articles, Snapchat Stories, or TikToks.

What Is The Most Reliable Platform For Trading Cryptocurrencies?

There are several platforms available for trading cryptocurrencies, however some of the most prominent ones are as follows:

1. The Kraken 1.

If you are just starting off, then this transaction is ideal for someone in your position. It will direct you in the right direction and assist you in reaching your goal of being an experienced trader.

2. Bitfinex.com

Bitfinex is the finest choice for those who want to monitor interested buyers and sellers for their specific financial instrument since it allows users to do so. The program is one of a kind since it has unique sophisticated tracking features as well as roughly eight different variants in order typeset for each and every scenario set.

3. Bittrex Inc.

The primary objective of Bittrex is to reduce the amount of time required for the processing of transactions. The cutting-edge technology that it utilizes has the potential to drive up demand for cryptocurrencies, and in terms of safety, it is superior to most other platforms.

What is the most effective strategy for trading cryptocurrencies on a daily basis?

Day trading is when you trade your currency on the same day, and it may be highly successful or not profitable at all depending on how you do it. The following are examples of platforms that are useful for day trading:

1. BitMex Inc.

BitMex is one of the early platforms and was created in 2014; despite the fact that it only permits trading in Bitcoin, it was the first. On this website, Bitcoin payments and withdrawals are processed without any fees, which contributes to the site's ease of use. The user interface is quite straightforward, and users are only permitted to maintain a single account type. It is easy to understand and doesn't need much effort.

2. The CEX.IO

Using this platform, you will have the ability to trade your money against a variety of other fiat choices, including the US Dollar, the Euro, and the British Pound, among others. It provides both a basic trading platform, which consists of buying and selling for fiat currency, and an advanced trading platform, which enables you to establish limits and participate in margin trading. The basic trading platform allows you to buy and sell for fiat currency.

3. Whalewatching Club

Day traders use this site often since it is another one that caters to their needs. You will only be able to trade in cryptocurrencies using this platform.

The digital money is used for all transactions, including deposits and withdrawals. There is no cost associated with account activity or deposits; however, there is a nominal charge associated with withdrawals. In general, its trading is extremely specialized, and it is very simple to make use of.

How Does The Internal Revenue Service (Irs) Handle Cryptocurrencies?

The Internal Revenue Service considers cryptocurrency to be property. Therefore, if you are merely keeping cryptocurrencies without adding or subtracting any value, you won't be liable for any taxes since holding cryptocurrency is considered a passive activity. If you possess the currency for more than a year but less than two years, you are responsible for the long term capital gains tax. If you keep the currency for less than a year, you are responsible for the short term capital gains tax.

Other transactions that qualify as taxable events include selling your cryptocurrency, exchanging it for another currency, or making a purchase using the cryptocurrency in question; in each of these cases, you will be required to pay taxes. If you make a profit from the sale of your cryptocurrency, you are responsible for paying taxes on the gain.

What are some essential hints and recommendations for novice investors getting started with cryptocurrency?

You are making progress in the correct direction. Knowing practically everything there is to know about a subject, particularly one that is as big, sophisticated, and technical as cryptocurrencies, is unquestionably the most astute thing that one could do with their time. However, there are certain things that cannot be accomplished with merely the information gained through textbooks and classroom instruction, and one factor that sets novices apart from more experienced people is their lack of prior experience.

However, there is no need to panic just yet since the following advice and suggestions are simple to implement and might very well make you seem to be the seasoned bitcoin investor that you want to be eventually.

1. Make every effort to resist temptations.

If you prefer to kill time by snooping around digital currency exchanges, then the first piece of advice is going to be right up your alley. When consumers see one coin's price skyrocketing in comparison to the prices of other coins, they almost always have an immediate impulse to invest in that particular currency. The reality is that it is in your best interest to work against this sensation. It is likely that the coin will have already returned to its standard price by the time you have finished making the transaction or clicked the button to confirm the purchase. Therefore, giving in to temptation will only result in you having a wallet full of losing tokens after it's all said and done.

2. Don't bother attempting to forecast the unforeseen.

When compared to more conventional markets, the bitcoin market is characterized by much higher levels of volatility. It is for this reason that it is more practical to devote time into the market by trading and buying instead of merely predicting trends and basing judgments on inferences that are not very reliable.

3. You should only invest your ephemeral assets.

If the commander of an army is aware that he will need his troops to at least have a chance of winning the next fight, he will not place those men on the front lines of a conflict that they are likely to lose. In the same vein, you should not invest money that you cannot afford to lose (such as the savings you have set aside for your child's education), particularly in something that is clouded by an excessive amount of hazards. This protects you from going bankrupt in the event that your trading and investment activities   involving cryptocurrenciesdon't work out as well as you had hoped they would.

4 "Don't be a hodler"

Those who have been active participants in the cryptocurrency trading industry from its earliest years are well acquainted with the expression "all in one day." This phrase, which was initially a mistake on a forum, has evolved into not just a nostalgic private joke but also a piece of advise that's very useful for beginners. It literally means "Don't let go" in several languages. The ones who need to hear this the most are the ones who are becoming too thrilled to see their assets grow. There are situations in which day trading is not the best technique, such as when you need to experience the highs and lows of a coin. Day trading is not the best method since the alternative pays off more frequently.

5. Do not give in to any pressure to make a trade.

Peer pressure isn't simply a problem that's common among young people who experiment with substances like alcohol and drugs; it's also something that might be a problem for grownups who are just starting out in the cryptocurrency market. Because of this, it is essential that you give the green light to enter it before anybody else does. One need to have a certain amount of confidence in themselves at all times. In addition to the topics that have been covered up to this point, it is essential that you have a solid understanding of how to calculate the target level for profits and the stop-loss level for losses. That essentially implies that you should be aware of when it is the right time to invest in a coin and when it is the right time to sell it.

6. Be aware of the characteristics of a successful investment.

When evaluating a potential new investment in this sector, it is important to take into account the following four elements in particular. The token, the team, the technology, and the timetable are these. When it comes to the first option, token, bear in mind that the reason you will be investing in one is because you have high expectations that its value will continue to rise in the future. If a first inspection of a token does not reveal any possible uses for it, it is in your best interest to move on to another candidate. The group, often known as the pool, comes up next. Making the decision to collaborate with one is a significant step. You are obligated to confirm the members' identities in addition to determining whether or not the website in question is genuine. The third one, technology, refers to the apps that may be used with cryptocurrencies rather than the tokens of cryptocurrencies themselves. You should ask yourself whether or not their use of cryptocurrencies is savvy and appropriate. Will there be a market for this particular technology? Will it be to the benefit of the community if it is implemented? And finally, for timing, it is of vital essential that you acquaint yourself with the milestones of your investment project, so you may also plan your following moves properly.

7. Aim to establish a varied portfolio of investments

If you want to avoid losing out on any potential investment possibilities, you should make it a priority to invest in as many different types of businesses as you can, provided that you have the financial means to do so. You may choose to practice HODL, invest in exchanges, or have numerous staking wallets for various cryptocurrencies. Alternatively, you could choose to practice staking. If you enter a larger number of horses in the competition, you will have a better chance of coming out on top.

8. Complete the assigned tasks.

Even if you have access to a wide variety of websites that detail the specific techniques you should use, it is in your best interest to avoid always listening to this advice. Sound research, which you should do on your own, is the finest foundation for all of the choices that you will make about your future in relation to cryptocurrencies. Be sure to get a hold of all the relevant information before you create an educated opinion. Additionally, as was discussed before, online posts that seem to be advocating a certain currency or exchange a bit too much are most likely a sponsored piece. This is because sponsors pay to have their content shown on websites. Don't be sucked in by the hook. The completion of the study might help you become more confident in your own tactics.

Going Forward with It

You should already have the answers to the focal questions of this chapter committed to memory before moving on to a detailed discussion on Bitcoin, Litecoin, and Ethereum (which is where the real fun begins). It shouldn't be difficult to understand the meanings of various terms like "fiats," "exchanges," "pools," and "wallets."

You should commit a comprehensive checklist for a mining beginning pack into your mind so that you may refer to it in the future. You should also be able to explain how cryptocurrency trading works at this stage, as well as why engaging in such activity may be advantageous. In conclusion, a simple method to evaluate your comprehension of this chapter is to inquire as to whether or not you are able to suggest online services that may contribute to the expansion of the Bitcoin economy by facilitating a continuous flow of transactions. Are there any of these that you find difficult to reconcile? Don't worry;

we won't be moving on from this chapter any time soon.

Getting To Know Bitcoin, Litecoin, AndEthereum: Their Positives And Negatives

Bitcoin was first developed by Satoshi Nakamoto around nine years ago due to the fact that he had a vision of a world liberated from the troubles that are caused by established financial systems. Issues such as inflation are a direct result of banks printing money in the form of credit. This implies that in response to a request for a loan, actual physical money will be printed and sent to the borrower. A genuine asset, such as gold, ceased to provide any kind of backing for the currency. In the end, the production of an excessive amount of paper money resulted in inflation, which in turn resulted in an ongoing trend of rising product prices, which drove a growing number of people deeper into poverty. The truth about our current monetary system is as follows.

However, it's possible that this reality is going to shift. The one and only reason why this system has not been overturned at this point in time is because no one has been able to devise a superior replacement for it. To be truthful, there was an effort made to create a private currency that would be backed by precious metals. This money would have been called the "Liberty Dollar," and it would have been called that. However, due to the fact that it made the US Dollar weaker, it was not successful in moving beyond the first period of formation. However, they did acquire some knowledge as a result of that event. They came to the conclusion that in order for a comparable initiative to be successful, it could not have genuinely sprung from any one person or item. As a result, there is not yet any other option that can be used instead of fiats. That is, not until someone invented Bitcoin.

In this chapter, we will take a more in-depth look at three of the coins that are presently in circulation on the market that are considered to be among the most precious as well as the most popular. You will have the ability to know the benefits and drawbacks of each one, in addition to receiving short insights into the specific markets that each one serves.

You should be able to determine, with the assistance of the following questions, which of the Big Three cryptocurrencies — Bitcoin, Litecoin, and Ethereum – would be most suitable for your needs.

What are the benefits, in general, of purchasing cryptocurrencies or making investments in them?

What are some of the most common drawbacks associated with purchasing or investing in cryptocurrencies?

When it comes to purchasing or investing in Bitcoin, what are the benefits and drawbacks, if any?

Litecoin: what exactly is it?

What are some pros and downsides of purchasing or investing in Litecoin, and why would someone do either of those things?

-Can you tell me about Ethereum?

Buying Ethereum or making an investment in it: what are the benefits and drawbacks of doing either?

Are there any other cryptocurrencies than the Big Three that are interesting enough to warrant keeping an eye on?

INVESTMENTS AND

It is time to learn how to correctly invest in cryptocurrencies now that you have a rough concept of what they are and a few of the most important principles that revolve around them. Investing in cryptocurrencies comes with both benefits and hazards, and it is vital to have a clear understanding of both before delving into the specifics.

THE ADVANTAGES

The fact that it is available to anybody and does not demand a significant amount of money (in some circumstances) is the primary advantage, and it is also likely the most important one. Because of this, many more doors will be opened for more individuals, which means that it will be simpler for you to get into whatever it is that you are interested in (at least in theory). When it comes to investing strategies that are considered more conventional, it is customarily necessary to make a sizable initial commitment and have a deep understanding of the field in which you are investing. When it comes to cryptocurrencies, having a greater main amount is helpful; nevertheless, it is not really required. This is particularly true if you already own the necessary gear to begin turning your attention to mining.

Another significant advantage is that practically all financial dealings may be completed in real time and almost instantly be subjected to processing. This is beneficial for you since, with certain other types of investments, you might anticipate receiving your money a few days after making the investment. On the other hand, given how

Blockchainworks and how quickly transactions are completed, you should have access to your money in a matter of seconds at most.

Investing in cryptocurrencies will provide you with a high level of safety, which is yet another significant advantage you will enjoy as a result of doing so. Because the market is so diversified, there are many different options for you to invest your money without having to worry about fraud or other typical issues associated with internet transactions, such as loss of identity or credit or debit card information. Because the whole process is documented publicly, if you do run into an issue, there are various methods to determine who is to blame for it (unless the currency in question is exchanged in a manner that prevents this from occurring, like Dash, for example).

The fact that significant levels of flexibility are involved is the last advantage that you may appreciate, and it's certainly something to look forward to. Due to the fact that the whole of the market is conducted online, it has been exempt from regulation by a variety of countries and organizations. Because of this, the fees are also kept to an absolute minimum. Investing in cryptocurrency generally speaking is a free-for-all with very little competition for you to contend with.

RISKS

Despite the fact that there are a lot of upsides and advantages to investing in cryptocurrencies, there is also a significant amount of danger involved. When it comes to investing, it is essential to be aware of these potential dangers; doing so may help you preserve more money than you first anticipated being at risk of losing.

The fact that the market's behavior can never be predicted accurately presents the first and by far the most significant threat. Because of the unpredictable nature of the movement of cryptocurrency prices, nobody can guarantee that you will earn a profit from your investment in the long run. You could invest 50,000 United States Dollars in a fund, just to turn around and see the money vanish right in front of your eyes. Despite this, you shouldn't allow it dissuade you too much since the same concept applies to many other kinds of investments. It is crucial to look at trends in the market and educate yourself on what you will be investing in so that you can reduce the impact of this risk as much as possible.

The fact that it is not regulated presents yet another significant danger. It is possible to see this as a positive aspect since it confers a great deal of liberty; nevertheless, it also implies that there are no guidelines to follow. On the other hand, you must be careful not to confuse regulations with guiding principles. When it comes to investing and trading, there are a few guiding rules that you are supposed to adhere to. One of these ideas is to avoid double spending. If someone were to make two purchases using the same credit card, there is not much that can be done to stop them, and they may not even get in trouble for it.

The fact that it is difficult to generate money is the ultimate danger that you face. Large quantities of money will be required on your part if your goal is to invest and get a return that is satisfactory and allows you to maintain your current standard of living. If you decide to go the path of mining, there are a lot of start-up expenditures you'll need to include into your budget, on top of the fact that the whole process is fraught with uncertainty.

Although these three dangers account for the most of the challenges you'll face, it is essential that you familiarize yourself with any currency you end up investing in since every coin has its own set of dangers.

Ethereum (ETH)

Ethereum is a decentralized platform that is powered by the digital currency ether (ETH) and a large number of other apps. It is managed on a global scale.

ETH

Ethereum (ETH) is a kind of cryptographic currency. It is a minuscule amount of digital currency that may be used on the internet, similar to Bitcoin. In the event that you are new to the world of cryptocurrencies, the following is the primary distinction between ETH and conventional currency. With Ethereum, you may function as your own bank. It is not necessary to involve any third parties since you are able to demonstrate ownership of your possessions just by using your wallet. Even though web currency is relatively new, it is obtained using encryption that has a proven track record. This protects not just your wallet but also your Ethereum and any trades you have made.

You are able to transmit your ETH with almost no intermediary administration, like as a bank, required. It is quite similar to handing money over to another person in person, but you can do it securely with anybody, anywhere, and at any time. The Ethereum network is decentralized and operates globally. There is not a single institution or bank that has the authority to choose to print additional ETH or alter the parameters of its use.

To be able to recognise Ethereum, all you need is a web connection and a wallet. It is not necessary to have access to a ledger in order to recognize payments in installments. Because ETH is divisible up to 18 decimal places, it is not necessary to acquire 1 ETH in its whole. You may make a single purchase for all of the components you require, which will cost you only 0.000000000000000001 ETH. ETH is considered to be the "soul" of Ethereum. When you transmit ETH or use an Ethereum application, you will be required to pay a small fee in ETH to the Ethereum organization in order to make use of its services. This expenditure is an urge for an excavator to analyze and validate what you're seeking to achieve, and it's necessary in order to do so.

Miners are analogous to the record-keepers of Ethereum; they ensure that no one is cheating by checking and demonstrating that no one is. In addition, miners that complete this activity are eligible to get a compensation in the form of freshly issued ETH in restricted numbers.

What factors contribute to ETH's current market value?

ETH's are significant to different people in a variety of different reasons. ETH is essential for Ethereum users since it is the currency that can be used to pay the transaction fees associated with using Ethereum. Others see it as a digital asset with great value, due to the fact that the creation of new ETH will eventually slow down. This leads them to believe that it will retain its value over the long term.

In recent months, ETH has emerged as a key asset for users of financial apps built on Ethereum. This is on account of the fact that ETH may be used either as a safeguard for crypto credits or as a payment structure. Evidently, many people also regard it to be an enterprise in the same way that Bitcoin and other types of digital money are ventures.

On Ethereum, cryptocurrencies other than ETH may also be traded.

On Ethereum, anybody is free to create new types of resources and trade them with others. These are referred to as 'tokens' in the industry. People have begun to tokenize traditional monetary standards, as well as their land, their crafts, and even themselves! There are a very large number of tokens that can be found on Ethereum, some of which are more useful and significant than others. Engineers are always developing new coins that unlock further prospects and usher in fresh market segments.

Intelligent Contracts

Brilliant agreements are digital agreements that are stored on a blockchain and are automatically implemented when certain predetermined conditions are satisfied. These types of agreements are referred to as smart contracts. Smart contracts are essentially computer programs that are stored on a blockchain and only activate when certain predetermined criteria are satisfied. They are often put to use to automate the process of carrying out an arrangement so that all of the participants may be immediately certain of the outcome, with almost little participation from go-betweens and minimal loss of time. They are also able to automate a work procedure, which will trigger the next action when the prerequisites have been satisfied.

Smart contracts are put into operation by adhering to standard language articulations that begin "in the event that..." and "when..." and are stored as code on a blockchain. When the predetermined requirements have been satisfied and validated, a group of PCs will take action and carry out the actions. These actions may include providing a ticket, delivering goods to the appropriate meetings, enlisting a

156

vehicle, or sending out alerts. When the cryptocurrency exchange is complete, a new copy of the blockchain is created. That means the transaction cannot be altered in any way, and the only parties who may see the results are those who have been given permission to do so.

In a good agreement, there may be as many expectations on a case-by-case basis as are necessary to reassure the parties involved that the project will be completed in a manner that is mutually satisfactory. Members should determine how exchanges and their information will be handled on the blockchain, come to an agreement on the "if/when...then..." decisions that will govern those transactions, study every possible special circumstance, and define a framework for resolving problems before the terms can be laid down.

A designer would then be able to make changes to the brilliant agreement at this point; however, increasingly, organizations that use blockchain for business are giving formats, online interfaces, and other web-based instruments to rearrange structuring brilliant contracts.

Uses for Electronically Signed Contracts

By increasing the transparency of the inventory network, Sonoco and IBM are working to reduce the number of problems that arise when transporting life-saving medications. Pharma Entrance is a blockchain-based platform that is fueled by IBM Blockchain Straightforward Stockpile. This platform records temperature-controlled medications as they move through the inventory network to provide reliable, solid, and accurate information to a variety of different gatherings.

The Home Terminal is able to swiftly settle disputes with vendors by using smart contracts stored on the blockchain. They are creating more solid relationships with suppliers via continuing contact and improved visibility into the production network. This is resulting in more opportunities for basic employment and progression.

www.ingramcontent.com/pod-product-compliance
Lightning Source LLC
Chambersburg PA
CBHW071645210326
41597CB00017B/2121